I0817139

HISTORY OF BASKETBALL

KENNY ABDO

Fly!
An Imprint of Abdo Zoom
abdobooks.com

abdobooks.com

Published by Abdo Zoom, a division of ABDO, P.O. Box 398166, Minneapolis, Minnesota 55439.

Printed in the United States of America, North Mankato, Minnesota.
052019
092019

THIS BOOK CONTAINS RECYCLED MATERIALS

Photo Credits: AP Images, Everette Collection, Granger Collection, Icon Sportswire, iStock, Redux Pictures, Shutterstock, ©Gerry Broome/AP/Shutterstock p6, ©David Maxwell/EPA/Shutterstock p19
Production Contributors: Kenny Abdo, Jennie Forsberg, Grace Hansen
Design Contributors: Dorothy Toth, Neil Klinepier

Library of Congress Control Number: 2018963564

Publisher's Cataloging-in-Publication Data

Names: Abdo, Kenny, author.
Title: History of basketball / by Kenny Abdo.
Description: Minneapolis, Minnesota : Abdo Zoom, 2020 | Series: History of sports | Includes online resources and index.
Identifiers: ISBN 9781532127380 (lib. bdg.) | ISBN 9781532128363 (ebook) | ISBN 9781532128851 (Read-to-me ebook)
Subjects: LCSH: Basketball--History--Juvenile literature. | Basketball--Juvenile literature. | Sports--History--Juvenile literature.
Classification: DDC 796.32309--dc23

TABLE OF CONTENTS

BASKETBALL

From packed arenas to driveways around the world, basketball puts the full-court press on every other sport.

DUKE
1

Whether it is a college or pro game, the rules stay the same. **Dribble** the orange ball down the court and shoot it into your **opponent's** hoop.

WARM UP

Canadian physical education teacher James Naismith is credited for inventing basketball. On a rainy day in 1891, he looked for a way to keep his gym class busy. And so, the sport was born!

Peach baskets were originally used for basketball hoops. They were replaced by string nets in the early 1900s.

There were nine players on each basketball team at first. It was based on the number of players on a baseball team. Teams were later reduced to five players on the court.

12

The National Basketball **League** was created in 1937. The Basketball Association of America (BAA) was founded in 1946. They merged in 1976 to make the National Basketball Association (NBA).

The Women's National Basketball Association (WNBA) was formed 20 years later.

BIG SHOW

Wilt Chamberlain holds the NBA record for the most points scored in a single game. He alone racked up 100 points against the New York Knicks.

100

Phoenix Mercury's Diana Taurasi was voted the best woman basketball player of all time by ESPN in 2017. Her skills playing for UConn, the WNBA, Turkey, and Russia helped her **clinch** the title.

LeBron James is considered one of the best players in basketball history. He has led his team to the NBA **Finals** in every **season** between 2010 and 2018!

35

The Golden State Warriors were the 2018 NBA **Finals** champions. They beat the Cleveland Cavaliers in four out of four games. Warriors small forward Kevin Durant was named Most Valuable Player (MVP) averaging 28.8 points per game.

GLOSSARY

clinch – to confirm a win.

dribble – bouncing the ball on the floor to advance down the court.

Finals – the championship series of the NBA where the team who wins best-of-seven games is determined champions of the year.

league – a group of teams that compete against each other.

opponent – a rival team.

season – the portion of the year where certain games are played.

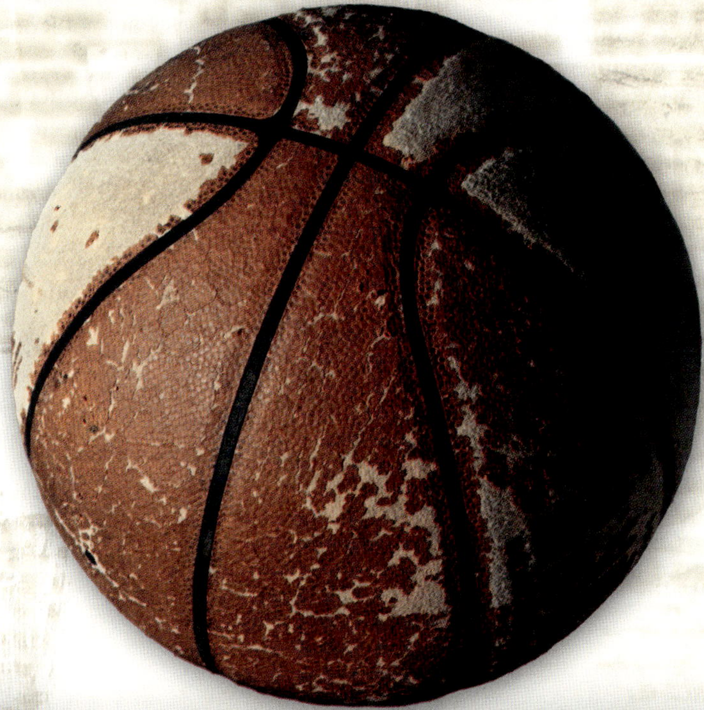

ONLINE RESOURCES

To learn more about basketball, please visit abdobooklinks.com or scan this QR code. These links are routinely monitored and updated to provide the most current information available.

INDEX